W9-BJM-643

Little Skill Seekers

BASIC CONCEPTS

SCHOLASTIC

New York • Toronto • London • Auckland • Sydney • New Delhi
Mexico City • Hong Kong • Buenos Aires

No part of this publication may be reproduced in whole or in part, or stored in a retrieval system, or transmitted in any form or by any means, electronic, mechanical, photocopying, recording, or otherwise, without written permission of the publisher. For information regarding permission, write to Scholastic Inc., 557 Broadway, New York, NY 10012.

Cover Design: Tannaz Fassihi
Cover Illustration: Michael Robertson
Interior Design: Mina Chen
Interior Illustration: Doug Jones

ISBN: 978-1-338-25558-4
Copyright © Scholastic Inc. All rights reserved. Printed in the U.S.A.
First printing, June 2018.

2 3 4 5 6 7 8 9 10   40   24 23 22 21 20

Dear Parent,

Welcome to *Little Skill Seekers: Basic Concepts*! Critical thinking is important for cognitive development and mathematical reasoning—this workbook will help your child develop this skill.

Help your little skill seeker build a strong foundation for learning by choosing more books in the Little Skill Seekers series. The exciting and colorful workbooks in the series are designed to set your child on the path to success. Each book targets essential skills important to your child's development.

Here are some key features of *Little Skill Seekers: Basic Concepts* and the other workbooks in this series:

- Filled with colorful illustrations that make learning fun and playful

- Provides plenty of opportunity to practice essential skills

- Builds independence as children work through the pages on their own, at their own pace

- Comes in a perfect size that fits easily in a backpack for practice on the go

Now let's get started on this journey to help your child become a successful, lifelong learner!

—The Editors

Draw a red circle around the cat.

Draw a blue square around the turtle.

Draw a green triangle around the bird.

© Scholastic Inc.

**Draw a blue hat
on the mouse.**

**Draw a yellow kite
for the boy.**

**Draw three red balloons
for the girl.**

**Draw a green ball
near the snail.**

© Scholastic Inc.

Circle the pictures that are the same in each set.

© Scholastic Inc.

Circle the picture that is different in each set.

© Scholastic Inc.

Circle the picture in each set that does not belong.

© Scholastic Inc.

Draw an arrow to show where each picture belongs.

© Scholastic Inc.

Draw a circle around each rectangle shape.

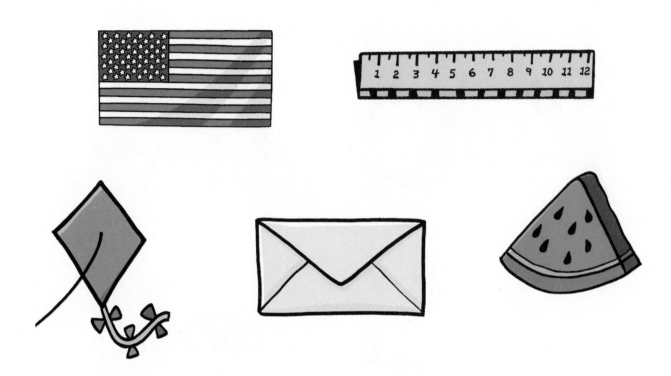

Draw a square around each oval shape.

© Scholastic Inc.

Draw a rectangle around each circle shape.

Draw a triangle around each square shape.

© Scholastic Inc.

Draw a circle around each diamond shape.

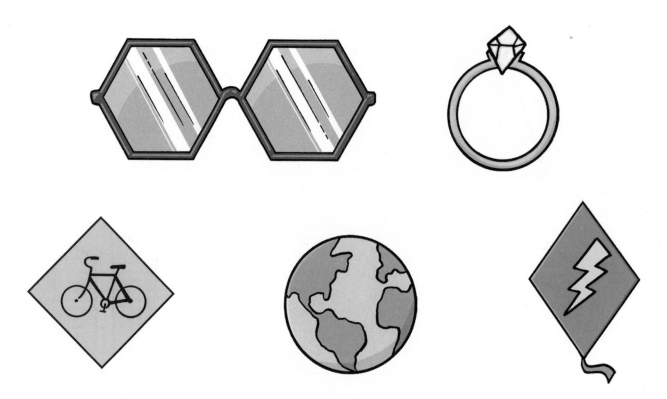

Draw a square around each triangle shape.

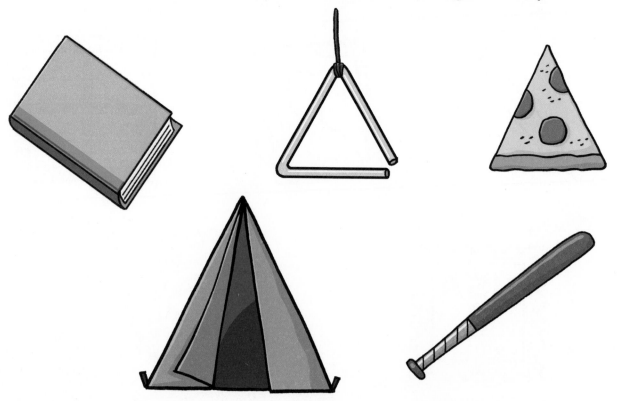

© Scholastic Inc.

Match the pictures with the same shape.

© Scholastic Inc.

Circle the picture that is big in each set.

© Scholastic Inc.

Circle the picture that is small in each set.

© Scholastic Inc.

Which objects are about the same size in real life?
Draw a line to match the pictures.

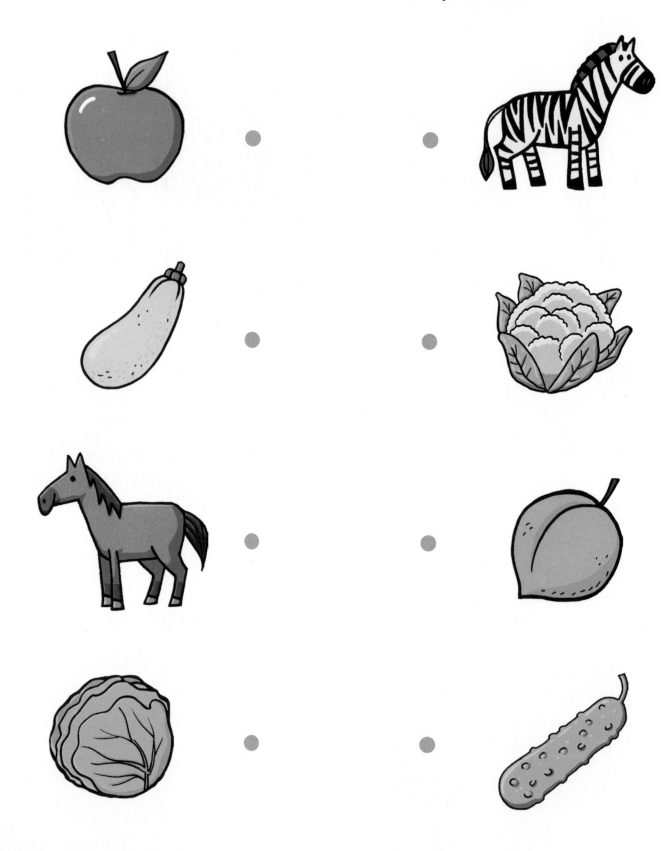

© Scholastic Inc.

Compare the pictures in each row.
Write 1, 2, and 3 to order the pictures by size.

© Scholastic Inc.

Circle the tallest person in the group.

Circle the shortest person in the group.

© Scholastic Inc.

Compare the pictures in each row.
Write 1, 2, and 3 to order the pictures by height.

© Scholastic Inc

Circle the animals that are in their homes.

© Scholastic Inc.

Circle the animals that are outside of their homes.

© Scholastic Inc.

Circle the book on the top.

Circle the hat on top of the boy's head.

Circle the child at the bottom of the stairs.

Circle the squirrel at the bottom of the tree.

© Scholastic Inc.

**Draw a square
above the alligator.**

**Draw a circle
above the kangaroo.**

**Draw a triangle
below the hippo.**

**Draw a rectangle
next to the quail.**

© Scholastic Inc.

Compare the sets in each row.
Circle the set that has more.

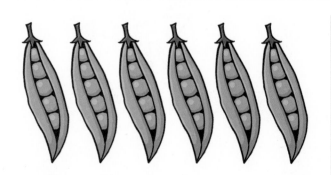 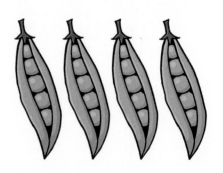

© Scholastic Inc.

Compare the sets in each row.
Circle the set that has fewer.

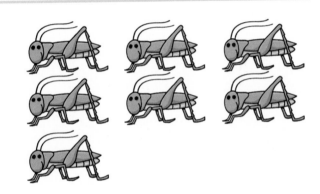

© Scholastic Inc.

Give each dog the same number of spots as its friend.

 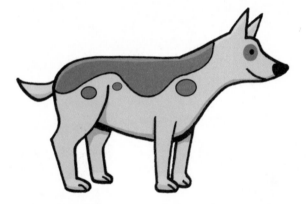

© Scholastic Inc.

Match the sets with the same number of objects.

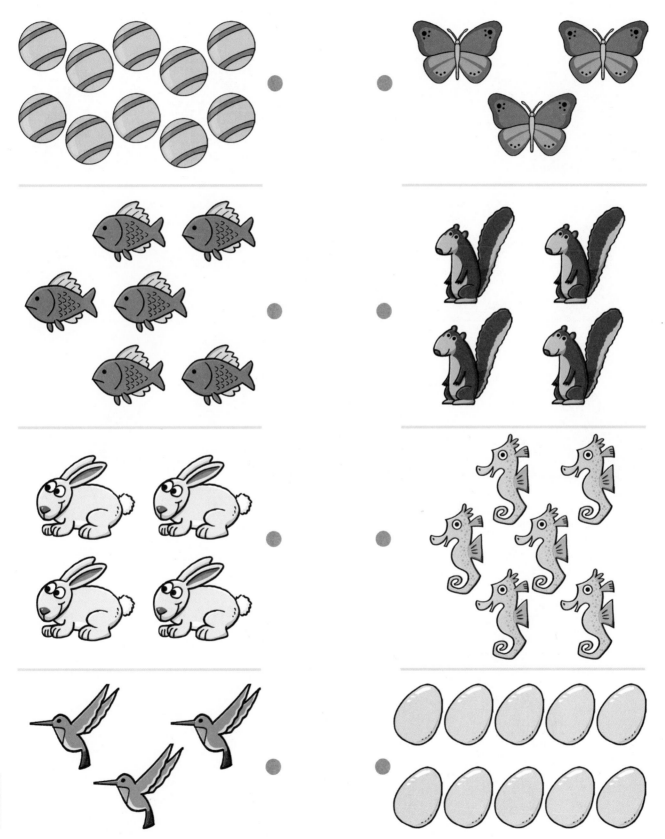

© Scholastic Inc.

Count each shape.
Color one box in the graph for each shape.

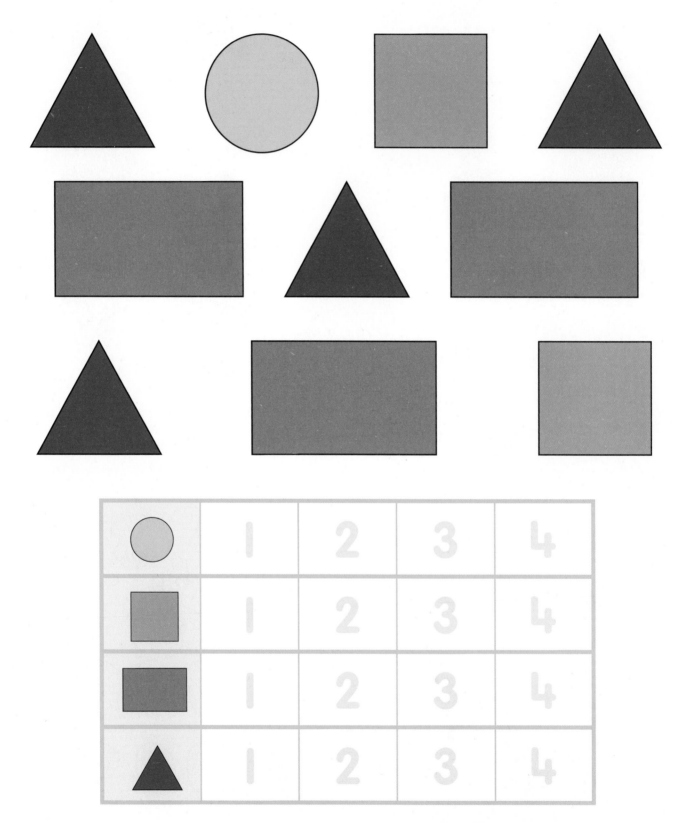

© Scholastic Inc.

Count each type of flower.
Color one box in the graph for each type of flower.

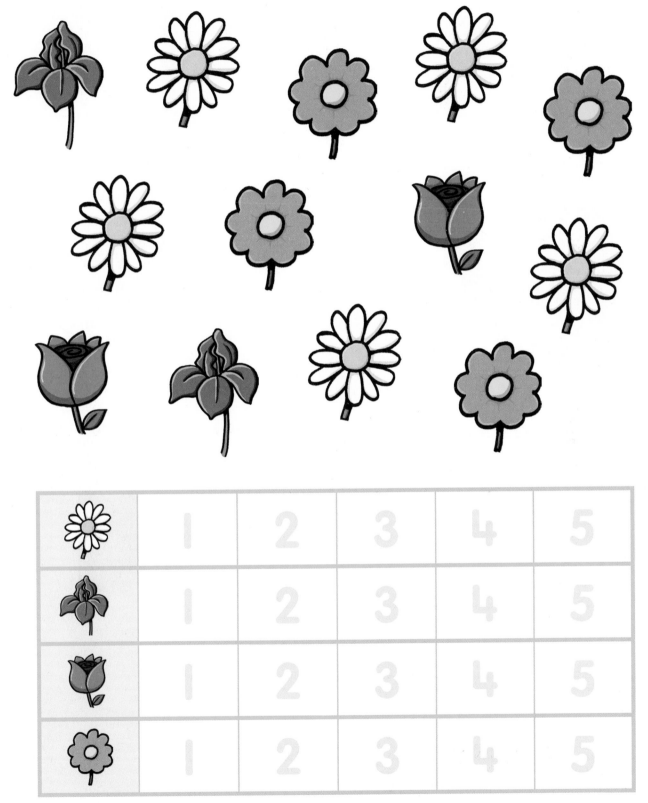

© Scholastic Inc.

Match the pictures that are opposites.

© Scholastic Inc.

Circle the picture that shows the opposite.

© Scholastic Inc.

What happens first, next, and last?
Write 1, 2, and 3 to show the order.

© Scholastic Inc.

Show the order of the story. Write 1, 2, 3, 4, 5, and 6.
The first one is done for you.

© Scholastic Inc.

Match the shapes that fit together.
The two shapes will make a square.

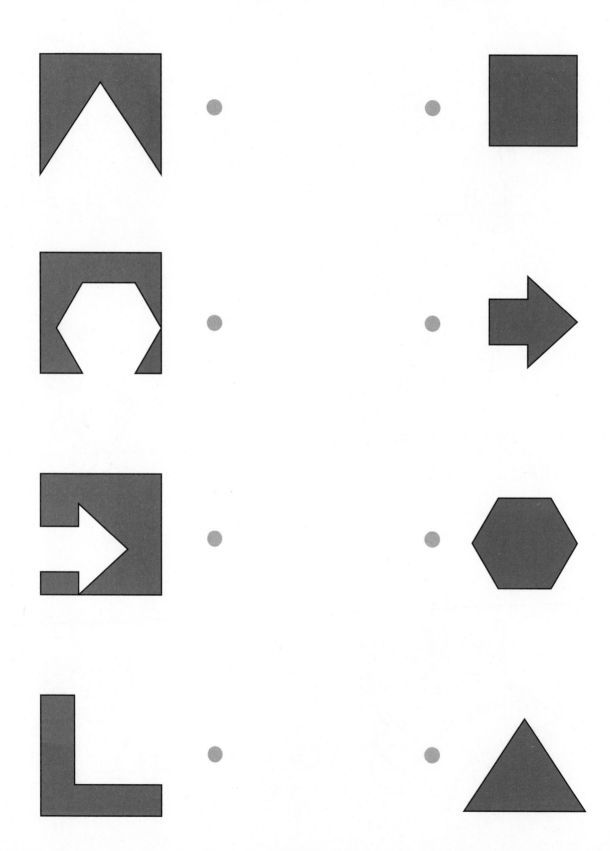

© Scholastic Inc.

Each boxed shape is missing a piece.
Match each shape to its missing piece in the center.

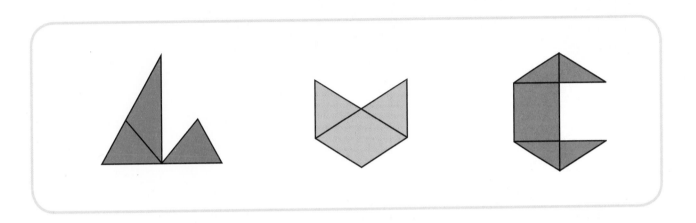

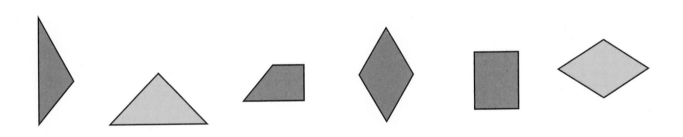

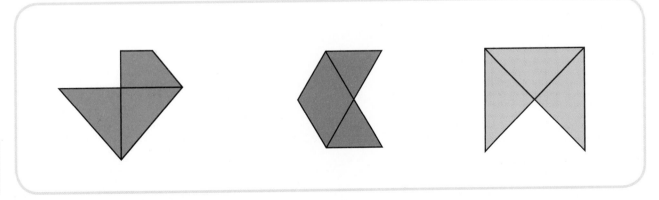

© Scholastic Inc.

What comes next? Draw it!

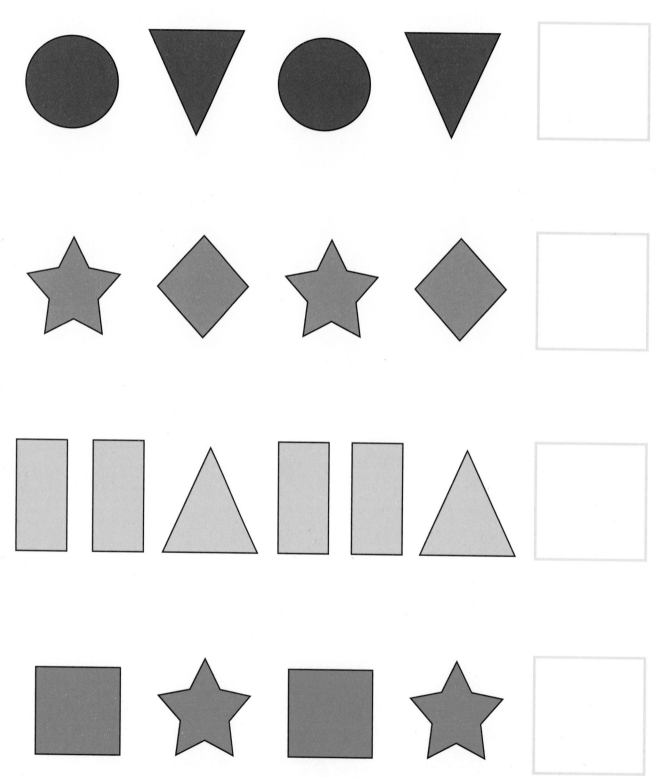

© Scholastic Inc.

What comes next? Draw it!

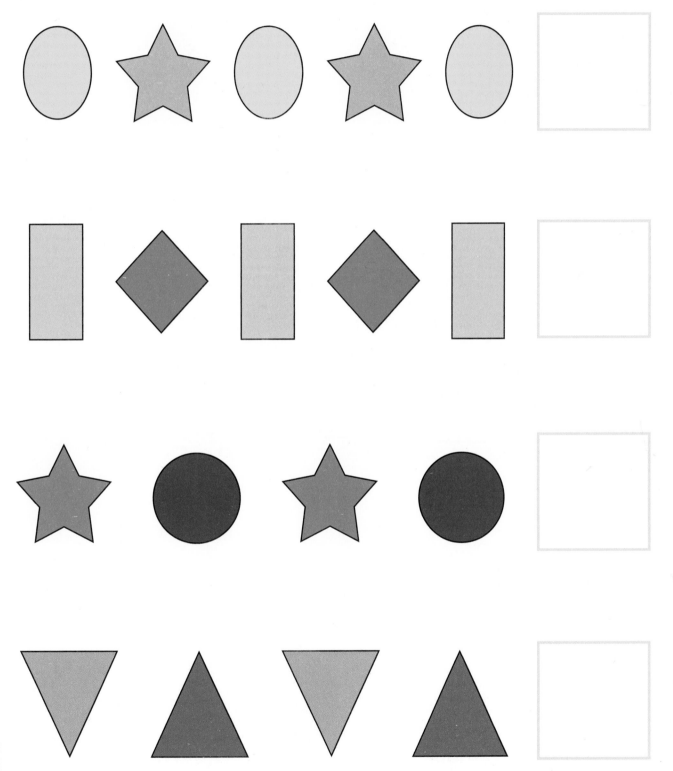

© Scholastic Inc.

37

Draw the missing shape.

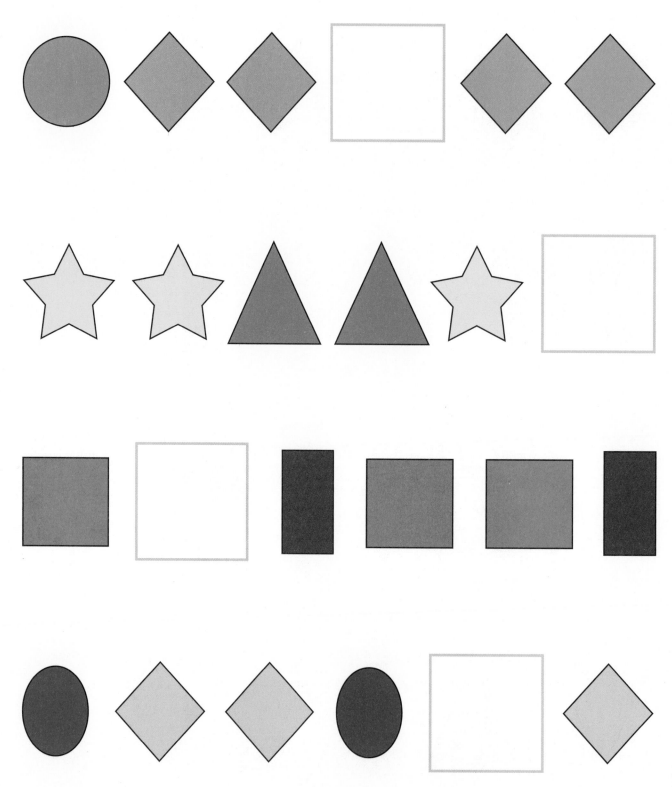

© Scholastic Inc.

Draw the missing shape.

© Scholastic Inc.

Draw stars to complete the grid.
Each row, column, and minigrid should have one of each color.

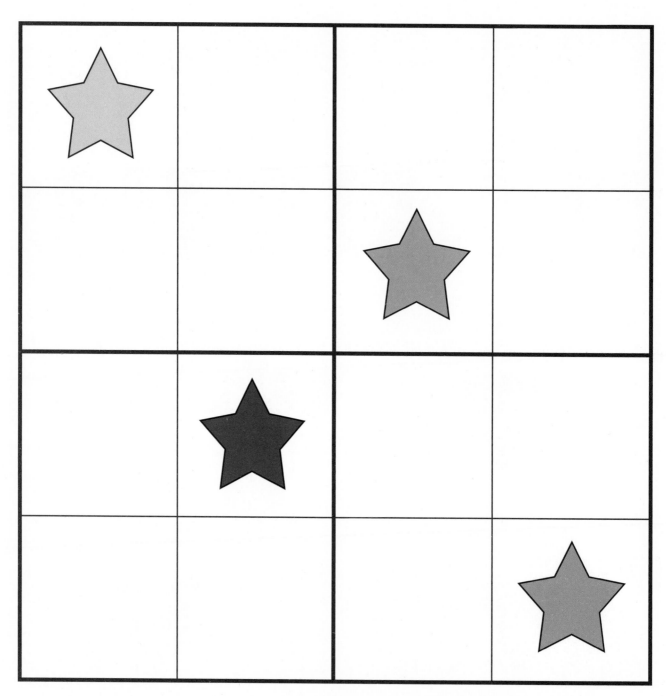

© Scholastic Inc.

Color the squares to complete the grid. Each row, column, and minigrid should have one square of each color.

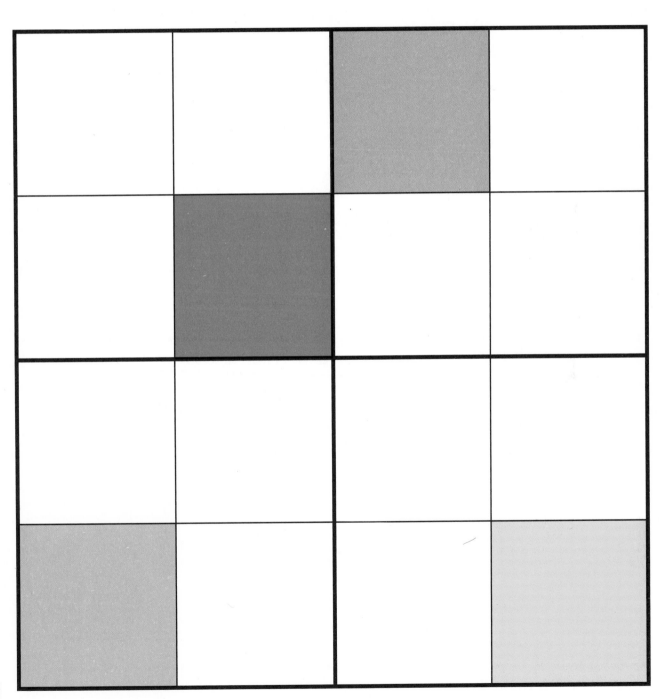

© Scholastic Inc.

Draw shapes to complete the grid.
Each row, column, and minigrid should have one of each shape.

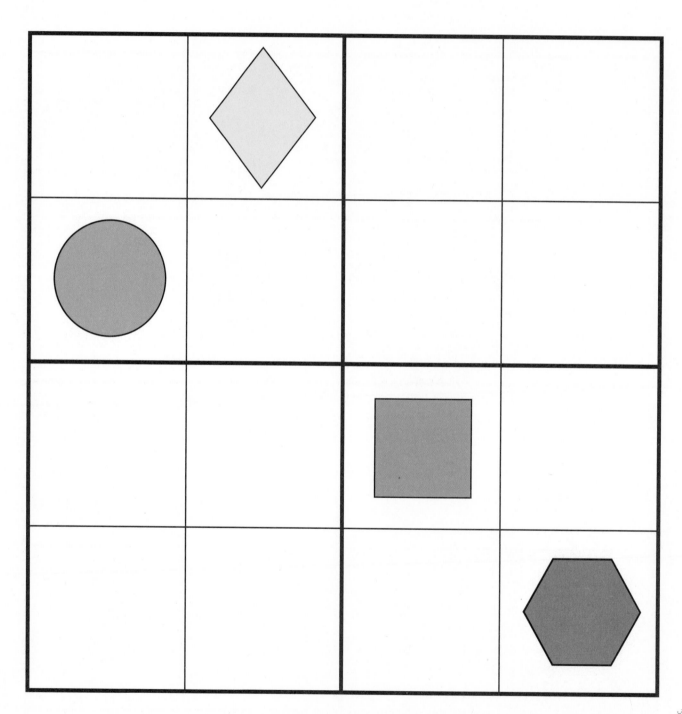

© Scholastic Inc.

Draw balls to complete the grid.
Each row, column, and minigrid should have one of each color.

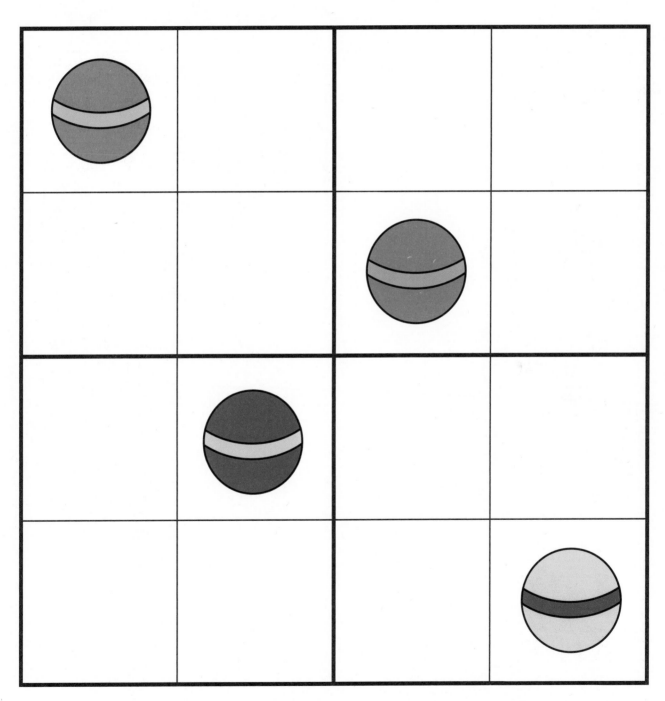

© Scholastic Inc.

Find and circle each item in the big picture.

© Scholastic Inc.

Find and circle each item in the big picture.

© Scholastic Inc.

Find and circle 5 pretend things in the picture.

© Scholastic Inc.

Find and circle 5 pretend things in the picture.

© Scholastic Inc

Answer Key For pages not shown, please check your child's work.

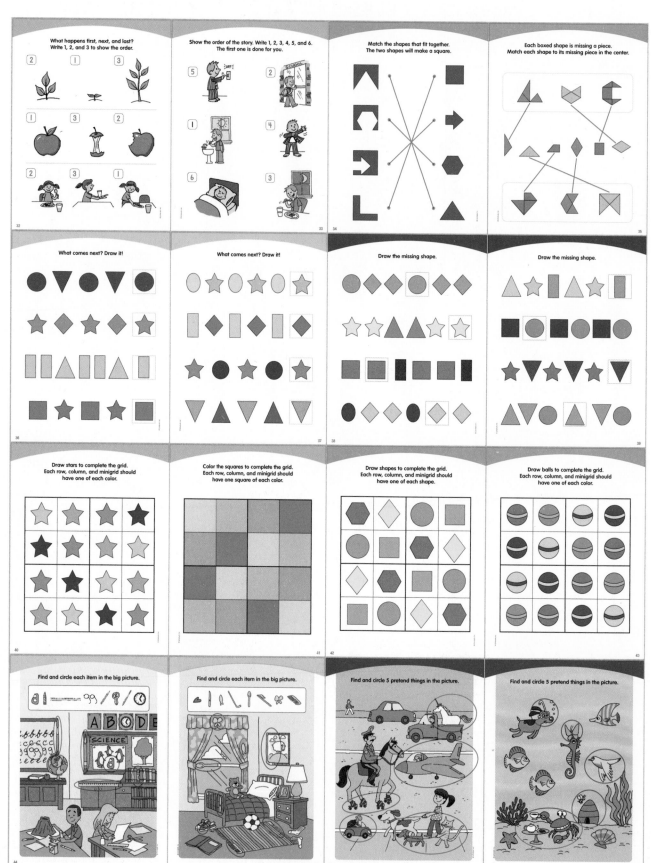

© Scholastic Inc.